Contents

W9-AHB-445

LEARNING TO PRAY FOR THE FIRST TIME— AGAIN!

Matthew 6:9-13

It is not uncommon to pray for something and then actually receive it. It is not uncommon to pray very hard and long and *not* receive what the heart desires. Some people are eager to share their experiences of answered prayer, while others keep to themselves their disappointment with God.

When our first son was five, he expressed a most direct feeling about prayer: "Why doesn't God give me what I want?" When I was twenty-five, I took God to task in my prayers because my grandmother had died. These kinds of prayers are never far from the Christian's lips.

Even when we believe we have demonstrated a consistent cause and effect for a particular answer, true prayer remains a mystery, as the "particulars" change from time to time and person to person.

O ye of little faith! The One to whom we pray may not follow through with any answers other than love, mercy, and grace; no answer, other than "My grace is sufficient for you." Here the real results of prayer will amaze and astound: "Prayer does not change God; it changes the one who prays."

Change us, O God immortal, from those who ask only for answers into those who pray for better questions. Amen.

Hymns: "Great Is Thy Faithfulness"
        "Sweet Hour of Prayer"

A NEW ATTITUDE

Philippians 2:5

J esus entered Jerusalem to the acclaim of thousands seeking the Messiah. This provoked the religious authorities who saw him as a competitor. The political powers feared a possible revolution. The inevitable conflict followed to the point of his arrest and execution.

In the end, would he become a martyr for Israel's freedom, or would he become the king of Israel who resisted his foes with force? Jesus sought neither outcome. Jesus "models" for all of us who come after him a new "human possibility." The power of God is released in the force of forgiveness.

As Evagrius Ponticus, the Turkish Christian mystic, instructed Christ's followers centuries later, "Do not allow the Devil to rejoice two times. You are sinned against and the Devil rejoices. Should you seek revenge and refuse to forgive, the Devil gladly rejoices two times. You are in his camp at last!"

When our own hours of affliction and oppression come, let us pray for a Christlike attitude. We forgive or we perish along with our enemies.

When the inevitable bad attitudes steal in upon us and the devil sees a triumph, tell us again the stories of Jesus. Amen.

Hymns: "Freely, Freely"
       "I Love to Tell the Story"

TRAVEL PLANS

Mark 11:15-19

Ask the next person you meet about any future travel plans. Soon you will be hearing about distant cities, countries never before visited, famous places. For some, an exotic foreign land awaits. A second honeymoon beckons a happy couple. Others are drawn to visit the country of their family's origin.

Such places will take on heightened emotional significance as the day of the journey draws near. Cameras are loaded, diaries are packed in suitcases, wills are even revised. The hour is at hand.

And so it was for Jesus and his band of disciples, his extended family, his travel companions. Before them lay Jerusalem, the ancient city of their ancestor David. Within its walls was the temple, the very center of the history of Israel! Any journey toward the center of one's family and personal history is full of possibilities! What might be found near the center of who we are and where we have come from?

Have you found the sacred centers in your pilgrimage of faith? Where is the "Holy Land" for you this day as you set out? What promise does your "Jerusalem" hold forth? Have you made your reservations?

All these questions are to help you make out your "to do" list before you set off on your journey. Being prepared is at least half the trip. The rest is up to your "travel guide." Remember, he's been there before!

Lord, may we travel light, so that our attention is on the destination, not on what we take along for security and comfort. You will attend to those as well, if we set our sights on the Land so close we can almost see it! Amen.

Hymns: "This Is a Day of New Beginnings"
       "He Leadeth Me"

FOREST PHYSICS AND GOD

Psalm 116:1-9

All students of classes like Physics 101 will remember the puzzler "If a tree falls in the forest and no one is there, does it make a sound?" The intent of the question is to help us understand the nature of sound waves and human senses.

To the student of faith there is a deeper question: "If a tree falls in the forest, does anyone care?" Is nature merely a series of phenomena with no ultimate purpose, no rhyme or reason? No! We believe that God's love encompasses the falling tree, the changes of seasons, the birth, life, and death of countless creatures, human and nonhuman. Even if no one hears, sees, or knows, there is love, because in God's purposes, to exist is to be loved.

Psalm 116 tells us that God's ear is inclined to hear the crown of creation, the human being. God's ear is inclined to all creation. The Lord has heard the voices of both gladness and sorrow. Even when no one else hears, God does; even when a single leaf falls, God knows; even when the end of all appears, God brings about a "new creation." God knows more than the physics of the forest; God knows the "physics" of love!

Grant that each that is and will be may come to trust your presence in all that rises, even though it falls in due season. And Lord, grant that all who fall, fall into you. Amen.

Hymns: "God of the Sparrow, God of the Whale"
"Fairest Lord Jesus"

CRYING ABOUT HEAVEN

1 Corinthians 15:21-28

Death, judgment, heaven, and hell are spoken of as the four last things. They tend to be interpreted chronologically, since it is easier to express life's beginning and ending in notions of time. Some theologians, though, imagine these last things as being more like the layers of onion. We can expect some tears as the layers are peeled away.

The tears that surround death and judgment are obvious: the former tells us we are mortal, the latter reminds us that our lives will be reviewed for both the good and the bad we have brought forth. When we think of hell, we become sorrowful as it brings up images of separation and isolation.

But crying over heaven? Well, who hasn't cried for joy? At the center of the onion, and at the center of our lives, is the heart of all creation, the Christ who makes us weep for joy unbounded! Only in Christ will all be made alive, every sin forgotten, every tear wiped away.

Doesn't it make your eyes water?

O loving God, may our tears flow freely for many reasons in this world, but for only one reason in heaven—joy unending! Amen!

Hymns: "Joy to the World"
　　　　"When We All Get to Heaven"

HOW TO DEFEAT THE MANY

John 2:13-22

When Jesus cleansed the temple by driving out the profit-minded money changers, he antagonized the religious authorities. Furious, they demanded a miracle to prove that his actions had divine authority.

His response? He spoke of raising a destroyed temple in only three days. This baffled his opponents. The disciples, though, heard a concealed message to be understood at a later time.

Did Jesus pull his punch against the authorities? The money changers felt his anger, so why not the ones who were the most dangerous to Jesus?

Perhaps the real marvel that day was the restraint Jesus exercised in not revealing his divine power. He was determined to allow the sacred drama to unfold, not wanting to reveal everything of God's plan prematurely.

Here it is enough to speak with divine authority before those who challenge the rule of God in our lives. Eventually, those who have the eyes of faith will see the miraculous in this "human temple," subject to crucifixion and cruel death. God acts by not acting as Christ is killed, but the last act of this drama is still under way!

Lord, when our prayers demand you to be a miracle worker, speak to us of human temples, dark tombs, and divine timing. Timing is everything, isn't it, Lord? Amen.

Hymns: "What Wondrous Love Is This?"
       "Seek Ye First the Kingdom of God"

DISCIPLES ARE MADE, NOT BORN

Mark 1:16-20

Jesus' call to discipleship is clear. A full, uncompromising commitment is asked. Mark shows us the call along the shore as Jesus beckons four rugged fishermen. Two sets of brothers eager to go with this new master respond immediately. Do they look promising?

Surely, if you were choosing a group of followers, wouldn't you be a bit cautious about two sets of brothers? Brothers fight among themselves. And wouldn't each set be competitive and envious of the other set? "Did not Jesus pick us first?" Mark later tells us that our suspicions were correct. Peter eventually became unreliable, and the sons of Zebedee asked for positions of power and prestige.

Perhaps this is one of the ways God shows that all of us are utterly human, susceptible to everything that ails our weak, creaturely nature. Even the best of disciples can't be too sure about their faithfulness. Will we really be there when God needs us? Remember the actor Gary Cooper in the movie *High Noon*? Did any town folk help him when the train rolled into town? When you watch that movie, look for the "disciple" characters. They are there. We are there also. Can we ever be trusted to be the followers who really follow through?

O gracious God, who really does call us personally, it is amazing that you are slow to anger, abounding in mercy, and more than willing to bear with us when we are weak. Thanks be to you. Amen.

Hymns: "Amazing Grace"
　　　　"Jesus Calls Us"

GOD *IS* HOME

Psalm 46

Though the earth should change . . . though its waters roar . . . though the mountains tremble"—God is our stronghold!

We expect some changes as life flows forward, through adolescence to adulthood, from singleness to marriage, from parent to grandparent. It's the unexpected changes we dread. There are the threats to our peace and security we try not to think about. These changes pull and tear at the walls of the only "home" we know—life.

Yet, this home comes with the promise that in the midst of all changes, even those that shake us with the fury of an earthquake, God is always there—our shelter and our refuge—a foundation that stands firm when all around it crumbles and falls.

A refuge is a habitation, a home, a place with which we have become familiar and to which we are even given a key! Here we are always welcome, and those within are like family. God is here. God is home! No foreclosures, no "loss of property value," no need for burglar proof security systems. A home certainly not made with human hands. God is here! God *is* home! Relax, put up your feet, and give thanks!

Lord, we are perplexed, but not driven to despair; persecuted, but not forsaken; struck down, but not destroyed; for you are our refuge and our strength. Amen.

Hymns: "Guide Me, O Thou Great Jehovah"
       "God Will Take Care of You"

NEVER FAR FROM OUR DEEPEST CONCERN

Mark 9:2-13

At first glance we may not think too much about the appearance of Moses and Elijah with Jesus on the high mountain. One of the main points being made is that Jesus is shown to be in the same company as the Law and the Prophets. Here the disciples learn that Jesus is, at the very least, the equal of the greatest of the Old Testament figures. His transfiguration and the voice from heaven acknowledging him as the Son of God assure us further that we are indeed seeing and hearing of the presence of God in this man Jesus.

On reflection, we notice something deeper: the past, the present, and the future have come together on this mountain. Time has been transcended as the past of Moses and Elijah meets the future Jesus as he will appear at the end of time (described in the book of Revelation). We are astounded to realize how time-bound we are!

A young child, giving first thought to his own death, said to his mother, "But Mommy, I'll be afraid when I die because you won't be there." She gently replied, "Yes, I'll be there. Time, as we know it, will be over. In fact, when you die and go to heaven, I'll be there to greet you. Don't worry your heart about these things. You won't be alone, and I'll be there for you." This mother only echoes the reassuring words of our God, who does not desert those of old any more than those born tomorrow.

Jesus, remember me when you come into your kingdom. May I find joy with Moses and Elijah and my family both past and future. Praise be to the Creator, Sustainer, and Redeemer. Amen.

Hymns: "Jesus, Remember Me"
       "Lonely the Boat"

COMMON SENSE WISDOM

Proverbs 14:15, 16

Ordinarily, we don't use the expression "gospel truth" when speaking of the book of Proverbs. Here we find a treasure house of accumulated observation upon human behavior. There is both praise for the wise and scorn for the foolish. It is as though this book of the Bible is there to remind us of our human condition. We need it as a mirror to see ourselves honestly. Here we find that some behaviors are harmful and should not be repeated. Here we have a hint of the wisdom we find in looking toward Jesus, a man of wisdom, as depicted in his dealings with sinful, hurting human beings who are slow to learn from experience.

Humans still have a knack for forgetting what they know to be the better way. Such folly plays itself out each day, from the school playground to the corporate office to the golf course.

Two brothers were playing golf. After nine holes they paused to eat some sandwiches. By the time they had finished the course, Mike, the older brother, had begun to feel sick. "Probably those sandwiches," he moans. The younger brother, John, grabs another sandwich and declares, "No germ can live in this body. I just shot two under par!" Somewhere logic or wisdom or both had broken down. The next day Mike had recovered, but John had taken to the sickbed.

With a slight smile we might read from the ancient wisdom reminding each of us that "the fool throws off restraint and is careless." No sermon needed. Common sense shared and accepted can help from generation to generation.

O One who protects fools and children, show us the ways that make for wise living. Remind us to look to those who have shown us ways to protect one another, to honor our lives, and to provide for the next generation by not ignoring what others have learned by mistake and correction. Amen.

Hymns: "Great Is Thy Faithfulness"
　　　　"What a Friend We Have in Jesus"

GRAFFITI FOR GOD

Philippians 1:15-18

In our modern interstate, six-lane, mass-transit culture, we still may see the gospel proclaimed from bridges and overpasses. Driving along listening to the radio, many people give no thought to God, Christ, or the Christian life. Then, suddenly before their eyes is that same overpass or bridge that they have passed hundreds of times, with the crudely painted words, "Jesus saves." In some parts of the South, you can still see concrete crosses along the side of the road, telling us "Prepare to meet God." These are not part of organized church efforts to share the gospel in our multimedia age! Yet in all their unsophistication, such attempts at proclaiming the gospel cannot be met with ecclesiastical embarrassment and elitism. What is said is still true.

Paul also had concerns about the motives of some of the other missionaries of his time. Perhaps the motives of our contemporary graffiti artists are not so pure either. Still, we can rejoice as Paul did that "Christ is proclaimed in every way" (v. 18). Since there are many yet to be reached, we allow for many different ways to reach them.

Lord, forgive us when we forget to share the gospel. Remind us that your saving grace is for all and that everyone does not see and hear in the same way. May the words of our mouths and the meditations of our hearts be acceptable in your sight, O Lord, our God. Amen.

Hymns: "Go Forth for God"
       "Sweet, Sweet Spirit"

IN THE DOGHOUSE?

Matthew 18:1-7

Even with the best of intentions, adults can leave children with painful memories of the church. Dan Ramage tells of his childhood experience with his first-grade teacher. Each Monday morning, the teacher asked her students if they had gone to church on Sunday. Most had, but there were always some who had not gone for a variety of reasons: parental lack of interest, illness, lack of transportation, inclement weather. To the teacher, these reasons carried no weight to alter the dreaded punishment for not being in the Lord's house on Sunday! She had a wallet-size photo of each student. On her desk was a small cardboard doghouse. Any student who missed church on Sunday went straight to the doghouse. To first graders this was an embarrassment. They felt an acute sense of shame. Dan soon learned to lie about church attendance to avoid the shame of the doghouse. What a choice for a child to make—shame in the doghouse or lying!

Jesus has very strong words about adults who cause the "little one to stumble." Life in the church is important, but the question of who should go to the doghouse is addressed only to adults, to those who should already know the right way to live. Adults are not only to live that way, but to be very careful not to cause problems for those coming behind them.

O Lord, how often have we sinned against children of the household of faith? How often have we been attracted by the letter of the law and not the spirit? How often, O Lord, are we in need of repentance, confession, and forgiveness! Show us your way we pray. Amen.

Hymns: "Happy the Home When God Is There"
"This Is a Day of New Beginnings"

IS IT SIN?

Romans 14:1-6

Not long ago, LeNoir Culbertson, a clergywoman, was leaving the hospital after a pastoral visit. As she prepared to exit the parking garage, the parking attendant looked at her clergy parking card, thought for a second and then asked, "Is gospel music sinful?"

What a strange question to address to someone the attendant did not know and in fact had never seen before. Dr. Culbertson said she felt as if she were being asked to take part in an exit poll that one might encounter when leaving a voting booth. Moreover, the question itself was odd. Perhaps the attendant was from a foreign country and was hoping to get an opinion from a clergyperson on a subject that troubled him. Perhaps gospel music was not common in churches in his country. It is entirely possible that he had heard someone describe such music as sinful.

Dr. Culbertson was not in a position to hear him out at length, so she replied that she did not think gospel music itself was sinful, but that anything might be the occasion for sin if used improperly. Had time allowed she might have encouraged him to read Romans 14, which deals with differences in opinion within the community of faith. Here Paul says some things are not to be judged by others. There are differences of practice, differences of likes and dislikes. Who are we to judge our brothers and sisters?

Obviously, such questions emerge in every generation of believers, and some are never resolved satisfactorily in a way that builds up rather than tears down the unity of the faithful. Still, the question will be asked many times, Is it sinful? Pray for the wisdom to know when to say yes or no, or That's not for me to judge!

O just Judge of all, help us to see where our sin lies before we ask about that of others. May we be quicker to forgive than to judge. May we deal with sin by doing justice, loving kindness, and walking humbly with you. Amen.

Hymns: "Nothing But the Blood"
       "Help Us Accept Each Other"

WHERE OUR DREAMS MIGHT LEAD US

Matthew 2:13, 19-20

Some dreams are dreams of geography, places we know little of and will never visit in person. I recently had a dream in which I was carried by a tornado to Austin, Texas! I don't plan on ever being in Austin, and I certainly do not expect to arrive anywhere by a natural disaster! So, I'm left pondering what fear, worry, expectation, or desire helped shape this dream of travel by tornado! Or, perhaps I should recollect what I had to eat that evening!

Our dreams deserve our attention, however, so that they are still respected as being part of who we are and indeed where we may be going. No part of our life is hidden from God and no part can be excluded from having the potential to be used by God in guiding us into God's future. Dreams speak to those parts of us that we often hide from, as well as those dimensions that are hidden from us. In other words, none of us is fully aware. We do not and cannot know all there is to know about ourselves. When the windows to our hidden rooms open even partially, let us not be afraid to look in. God will be there also.

O God of the known and unknown, how different are your ways! How hidden are the details of your revelation to us. How free you have made us to respond to what you have shown us in Jesus Christ our Lord. Lord, may we have eyes to see and ears to hear. Amen.

Hymns: "Open My Eyes, That I May See"
        "Be Thou My Vision"

CLOSER THAN WE REALIZE

Acts 17:28

O bjects appear closer than they are." This is a familiar phrase seen by millions of front-seat passengers in late-model cars. Emblazoned on the right side-view mirror, the phrase cautions the driver to not underestimate the closeness of a vehicle about to pass on the right side. The wide-angle mirror distorts the perceived distance of the approaching vehicle. Such a mirror gives a better view on the right side at the expense of depth perception.

This automotive safety message suggests a truth of the Christian faith. God is always closer than we realize. Our experiences, both good and bad, often act to make God seem at a great distance, aloof, absent, uncaring. This is not the case. God is "a very present help in time of trouble." We exist only because of the very existence of God.

We should be quick to say that, unlike the objects appearing in the side-view mirror, God is not an object. God is the very source of all that is and that includes us—human creatures. God is always present to the senses. God is immortal, invisible, Spirit, not subject to definitive description. God is always closer than we realize, but God is always more than we can conceive. To say this is to speak of a mystery, but nonetheless, a mystery that comforts us and gives us a security for whatever objects in this life may threaten our well-being.

O God eternal, majestic and mysterious, yet merciful and loving, come to us who have limited vision of what is eternal. Come close in our darkness and give us peace. Amen.

Hymns: "Immortal, Invisible"
      "Holy, Holy, Holy"

NOT NECESSARILY THE LATEST!

2 Thessalonians 2:15

Mistakes in wording or spelling in printed pieces can be both amusing and confusing! A recent advertisement from a dentist read, "Teeth extracted by the latest Methodists." Dentistry by denomination!

Besides the humor of the misprint, another truth that is often painful to us who want to share the good news is the fact that in trying to utilize the latest methods of evangelism, we can lose sight of the message itself. We try to speak to each generation in a language that communicates, but we must be cautious in making the gospel simply the latest modern philosophy, wisdom, or psychology. The gospel does have roots; the good news does have a history!

One of our greatest modern Christian witnesses to the faith, C. S. Lewis, thought of himself as one of the "last dinosaurs," because he felt so much more at home in the ways the gospel was expressed in the Middle Ages, in contrast to the ways of the twentieth century. More often than not, modern theology was to Lewis merely the latest fashionable thought cut off from centuries of faithful witness. He spoke not of the "latest Christianity," but of "mere Christianity," the core of truth shared by all the saints both living and dead. Before we appeal to the latest theology, perhaps we should read what was the "latest" in the first, fourth, or sixteenth centuries!

O Lord, we pray for clear voices and a shared vision when we proclaim the gospel. May the modern words of our mouths and the inherited meditations in our hearts be acceptable in your sight. Amen.

Hymns: "I Love to Tell the Story"
       "Lift Every Voice and Sing"

NOT TOO OPTIMISTIC, BUT FULL OF HOPE

2 Corinthians 1:3-11

The old saying is still around, "Optimism is what allows the tea kettle to sing, though up to its neck in hot water!" But optimism may have its limits. If the heat stays on and the water dries up, the singing will soon stop.

Optimism is not identical with Christian hope. Some persons are simply optimistic by nature and others are less so, more inclined to a somber mood. They are subject to the very state Paul described: They are "so utterly, unbearably crushed that [they] despaired of life itself."

Hope, however, dwells within all believers, since its mark is not personality but the trustworthiness of God. God has promised to all types of personalities that the future is surely in the hands of the One who loves us and will never let us go. Just ask Paul, the blinded, the shipwrecked, the imprisoned, the one who endured a "thorn." Optimistic? Maybe. Full of hope? Undoubtedly.

Lord, fill each of us with the hope that does not depend on the degree of our optimism or the depth of our despair. Amen.

Hymns: "Precious Lord, Take My Hand"
       "My Hope Is Built"

A NO-NONSENSE CHURCH

1 Corinthians 11:17-22
Titus 3:9

J ust imagine! A congregation mature, wise, loving, reflecting on earth what is in heaven. No divisions, no controversies, inclusive and accepting. I could go on and on since there is no lack of ways to describe what a faithful church might look like. Of course, we also have many descriptions in Scripture of how the church fails to be the reflection of God's kingdom. The imperfect has yet to become the perfect. Misguided attempts abound, however well intentioned, only to be corrupted in due time by humans given over to greed, pride, and idolatry.

Still, this does not stop those who, after much frustration with church life, throw up their hands and declare their own "no-nonsense church." I've heard it described as a church that "won't tolerate fool-ishness." Hope springs eternal that it can be found, can exist. In some sense this has been the history of the Christian faith. This spirit is the spirit of the church always being reformed! It is the closest we may ever get to a "no-nonsense church."

Merciful and loving God, you see us as we are and as we can be. You accept us just as we are, but call us forward to new life in Christ. Command us, rebuke us, mold us, make us into your eternal image. For Christ's sake and the Kingdom. Amen.

Hymns: "Revive Us Again"
         "Have Thine Own Way"

SPONGE, ABSORB, SQUEEZE OUT

Hebrews 12:1

Imagine, if you will, a church with very limited access to scripture, no Sunday school curriculum, no multimedia aids, and very limited communication with other churches. You have imagined the first Christians! They were utterly dependent upon person-to-person awareness of the gospel. The gospel was heard proclaimed, enacted in the gestures and symbols of the worship experience, and learned from living and sharing the Christian life in community. How did this intimate beginning grow into the church that exists in all the world?

There are several ways to describe the growth and perseverance of the church. One image is that of the sponge that absorbs and squeezes out. We are made to "soak up—absorb," so to speak, that which comes to our senses. It stays within us unless it has a means to be released. The Christian hears, sees, experiences. The believer stores what has been received. Then, in both the community of faith and the world, it is "squeezed out" by the constant contact with people around us. What is absorbed cannot remain within. In fact, it is squeezed out by the very act of worship, wherein the community of the faithful responds to God in word and deed. Worship celebrates and actually enacts what it says it believes—that is, what it has absorbed! The church can exist without the latest educational techniques and communication inventions. If they are available, that's great, but if they are absent, remember that the church will always, "sponge, absorb, squeeze out."

O God, whose word ever goes forth, thank you that the gates of hell will not prevail against your people. From age to age, there always will be a witness, there always will be the gospel shared. Amen.

Hymns: "Pass It On"
       "Go, Make of All Disciples"

ON TAKING TIME

Psalm 90:12

R arely does a week pass that you do not hear someone say, "Oh, just take your time." The matter may involve returning a borrowed item, returning a phone call, or undertaking a task. The timeline, often so important in work, family, or community obligations, seems removed. We are generally glad to hear those words, "Take your time." But the unspoken message we might hear behind those words is, "Be responsible with the 'free' time you have been given. It is now YOUR time to do with as you please, responsibly or irresponsibly."

The time we have been given by God is a gift. We must treat it as a gift to be enjoyed with an attitude of gratitude. Some of our time each day should be devoted to the awareness of God, whether through our vocation, avocation, or devotion. In other words, "Take your time . . . for God."

Help us, O God of all time and space, in our living and moving and being to recognize the gift of time, which comes from you out of eternity. May we take the time to be with you. Amen.

Hymns: "Take Time to Be Holy"
       "I Want to Walk as a Child of the Light"

"MARKETING" FAITH?

Psalm 35:9

Most denominations and many congregations have learned to use the latest marketing and advertising techniques for church growth and evangelism. Television, radio, periodicals, and the newer forms of computerized media all offer forms of advertisement for "great, growing, exciting churches." This is done with combinations of sound and color and images unthought of throughout most of church history. Many people have been attracted to churches through such appealing promotions.

Yet, the greatest attraction of a church is still the impression its members make on those outside its fellowship. The most convincing witness to the world is a joyful, enthusiastic Christian. Saint Teresa of Avila once prayed, "God deliver me from sullen saints." So might our prayer be, even as we attempt newer and flashier media campaigns on behalf of the church.

Our prayers could begin and end each day by looking in the mirror! We should pray about how we present ourselves to our families, friends, coworkers, and especially strangers and visitors we encounter each week before our day of worship! A "sullen saint" in the Kingdom rarely will make a good witness to someone outside the Kingdom! A cold Christian heart is a poor witness in a cold, heartless world.

Help us all, O God, to bear a cheerful spirit as each day unfolds in the presence of others. Save us from bad attitudes through heartfelt gratitude. Amen.

Hymns: "Come, We That Love the Lord"
       "Rejoice, the Lord Is King"

THERE ARE NOT TWO GOSPELS!

Galatians 1:8-9

Keeping the gospel clean and simple is not a task for the weak of heart! At each age and stage of life, the possibility exists to mis understand the gospel of faith and forgiveness, the good news of God's reign in our lives through our walk with Jesus. Additions to the simplicity of our relationship with God in Christ abound in each generation. Each generation of Christians can be a "lost generation" regarding the clear communication of the Gospel.

Jerry Raines tells the true story of how his hobby of woodworking could unexpectedly attract the airborne! His electric saws were placed in a shed at the back of his yard. There he created wood products from scrap lumber. As he was sawing away one day, he noticed two red-tail hawks above. He also began to hear their distinctive high-pitched call. He looked for other birds of prey in the field nearby. He saw nothing that would keep their attention or evoke their call. Finally, he realized that the sound his saw made was eerily similar to their call! Screee! Screee! They had been attracted to a similar but false call.

Like these hawks, Christians can be lured to the sounds of "another gospel" if we do not take care to hear what we once heard in its original simplicity and purity.

Lord, may our ears hear and our eyes see how simple the good news is. Remind us that other voices calling us may not reflect the gospel of our Lord Jesus Christ. Forgive us when we listen to their siren call. Amen.

Hymns: "Jesus, Keep Me Near the Cross"
       "How Firm a Foundation"

ANGELS UNAWARE

Hebrews 13:1-2

Making my rounds through the intensive care unit of the hospital, I suddenly heard, "Hey, big guy!" The husband of a patient I did not know had just greeted me. Neither did I know him! At first I thought the call was directed to someone else, perhaps out of sight behind me. No, he seemed to be calling out to me. I had no recollection of having met this man. I was at a loss and only waved as I went on by the room and down the hallway. The obvious explanation was one of mistaken identity, and I could ignore this stranger.

But I was drawn back to the room. I had been greeted by a stranger and had in turn ignored what might have been an invitation. I wanted to know who was calling me. As it turned out, it was a case of mistaken identity. He thought I was the social worker. When he realized that I was a chaplain, he shared not one but two stories of his encounters with angels. One had saved his life in New York City. Years later in West Virginia, a stranger gave him directions for staying off a dangerous mountain road. That stranger had a brother in New York City!

These stories enlivened my day, and I left feeling as though perhaps an angel had brought the two of us together for the purpose of allowing him to share his story with a fellow Christian. God would have us share our faith stories in most unlikely places with the strangers who appear suddenly in our lives. Entertaining angels unaware! It does happen!

O God of the earthly walk, help us to be attuned to your presence through others, so that we might learn to share together the mystery of your work in our lives. Amen.

Hymns: "Angels We Have Heard on High"
 "He Leadeth Me: O Blessed Thought"

DRESSED FOR THE WEDDING OF THE LAMB

Matthew 22:1-14
Revelation 19:6-9

Making preparations throughout life is a requirement of being human. As totally dependent infants, someone is making preparations for our daily needs and our future possibilities. "Be prepared," recites the young Boy Scout as he learns one of the fundamental tenets of Scouting and of the adult life awaiting him. Be prepared.

Attending the wedding of friends in a distant state, my wife and I were given the task of driving the bridegroom to the church for the ceremony. He was splendid in his white tuxedo and white shoes. He was the man of the hour! But, as we admired him in his splendor, we quickly noticed he had not made a complete preparation. Through the thin summer-weight material of his trousers, we could see faintly the presence of red polka dots! Polka-dot boxer shorts! Had we not noticed his slight fashion indiscretion, he would have been the center of attention rather than his beautiful bride!

These passages from the Gospel of Matthew and the book of Revelation likewise remind us to be prepared for the wedding supper of the Lamb of God. We are to prepare—seriously—for an outrageously good time in the kingdom of God! We are all invited!

O God who creates and is creating, remind us to be prepared for your rule in every heart, your kingdom which has no end, the wedding party which never lacks for good things! Amen.

Hymns: "Rejoice, the Lord is King"
"I Want to Be Ready"

DEBTS WE OWE AND CAN NEVER REPAY

Galatians 6

We are all dependent on the many unknown, unnamed thousands who contribute to our safety, our health, our security, our knowledge—to virtually everything we call our well-being. We are not self-sufficient in having "life, liberty, and the pursuit of happiness." We do not and cannot save ourselves. We are all needy and dependent. We all owe debts to others we can never repay.

One way to express our gratitude for the work of the neighbor and stranger is to discipline ourselves to pray silently when we see someone in a work-specific uniform or attire—the policeman, the nurse, the coach, the teacher. Norman Vincent Peale used the image of directing "prayer darts" whenever using public transportation. He would direct these "prayer darts" toward the pilot, flight attendant, driver, whomever, as they carried on their tasks unaware that they were being supported and thanked for their work. This was often the only way he could say thank you, since he could not be in the actual presence of those rendering the service. In this simple, silent way, one acknowledges that debts are owed to many whose training, education, experience, and commitment make for a life less threatened by harm, illness, or discomfort.

O God, for the butcher, the baker, the candlestick maker; for the doctor, the lawyer, and the fire chief; for the nurse, the teacher, the coach; for the countless thousands to whom we owe our lives and our comfort, we give you thanks. Amen.

Hymns: "Take Time to Be Holy"
       "We Meet You, O Christ"

LEADERSHIP IS MORE THAN ONE

1 Timothy 3:14-15

Bill Bright, the founder of Campus Crusade for Christ, studied for many years in a seminary, but never felt called to be a pastor. He wanted to contribute as a leader and guide for the laity as a layperson!

He tells the story about a church whose beloved pastor retired after years of service in that one church. The congregation felt lost at first. They were without a pastor for months. Gradually, different ones began to take responsibility for seeing that the sick were visited, visitors received follow-up visits in their homes, and that other members were recruited for tasks within the congregation. A few people dared to preach, while others discovered they could lead a Bible study. The church began to attract new members and increased its worship attendance. New ministries to the community were begun by people who had gifts for communication, planning, and "getting the job done."

Eventually a new pastor arrived. The people gradually relinquished their shared leadership and became dependent upon the preacher, who wondered why the people hid their light under a bushel!

Although the story exaggerates the reality, most of us can see the painful truth—we all too readily become dependent upon the preacher to do the work of ministry.

Lord, send a revival, and let it begin with me. Amen.

Hymns: "Are Ye Able"
   "Rise up, O Men of God"

FOR THE BEAUTY OF THE EARTH

Psalm 90

Psalm 90 was written as the children of God began to rebuild the temple that had been destroyed by their enemies. In verses 16-17, the writer acknowledges the beauty that God created, and asks God's blessing on the building done by human hands.

Just for today, promise yourself that you will take time to really see and marvel at God's creation. It won't take as much time as you might imagine! You don't have to go to the mountains or the shore, you don't even have to leave your home or office or school. When you give thanks for the food you eat, take time to really look at and enjoy that food. Think of the many times bread is mentioned in the Bible. Recall Jesus' words about bread. Look around you—other people are part of God's creation—beautiful, varied, marvelous in God's sight! You're spending the day alone? Take time to really look at and marvel at your hands. Stand up for a stretch break and marvel at the wonder of your body. Give thanks to the Creator for this, the most wonderful creation. Remember the rebuilding of the temple, and remember Jesus' words comparing our bodies to temples.

God gave us these wonders of creation, and with them, God gave us the responsibility to care for all creation. If we take just a very few minutes each day to really look for signs and wonders, it will become much easier to accept that responsibility.

Lord, as little children we learned to say prayers of thanks, but now we often forget, making our prayers more often complaints. Hear us now, as with the faith of a child we say, "Thank you, God, for everything." Amen.

Hymns: "For the Beauty of the Earth"
"Joyful, Joyful, We Adore Thee"

JUST UNLUCKY?

Psalm 16

How often in a week's time do you say or hear others say, "That's just my luck!" or "I'm just unlucky!" or even "If it weren't for bad luck, I'd have no luck at all!"

The next time you're tempted to blame "luck," remember an old tale from the Brothers Grimm.

A merchant had done good business at a fair and, with his bag filled with gold and silver, started home. At noon he stopped to rest, and the stable boy noticed that his horse had lost a nail from the shoe of his left hind foot. Anxious to get home, and having only six miles to go, the merchant decided not to stop for the few minutes it would take to hammer in a nail. About halfway through the remainder of his journey, he stopped to water the horse and again a stable boy pointed out the missing nail. The merchant reacted in the same way—surely he could get the rest of the way, and so he rode off. But before long the horse began to limp, and then to stumble. Shortly after that the horse fell and broke his leg. The merchant had to leave the horse where he fell, unstrap the bag, take it on his back, and go home on foot.

"That unlucky nail," he said to himself, "has made all this trouble."

O loving God, you made us with the means of reasoning. Remind us that try-ing to do things too quickly, without giving thought, will certainly have an impact on our "luck." Amen.

Hymns: "All the Way My Savior Leads Me"
"Here, O My Lord, I See Thee"

SO BE ON YOUR GUARD

Mark 13

Mark 13 emphasizes one command: Be alert, watch! No less than five verses repeat the exhortation to be prepared for the turmoil and deceptions that lie ahead.

I can still hear Doc Hatcher, the father of a fellow Scout, telling our troop as we were leaving for camp: "Have a good time; be a good Scout. Be prepared."

His advice has stayed with me for more than thirty years, and I have followed it with varying degrees of success.

From the viewpoint of faith, our lives may not have been graced with a "good time"; most surely, our "good Scout" days have been more than equaled by our "bad Scout" days! And who is bold enough to say they have always been prepared? Few of us are consistent in following commands. Most advice received is advice eventually forgotten.

Faith, finally, is trusting that Someone else is better prepared than we are for what lies ahead.

Lord, we know that you are always with us. Help us to put our trust in you, so that we will always be ready for whatever the day holds. Amen.

Hymns: "Immortal, Invisible, God Only Wise"
        "Where He Leads Me"

ROOM FOR WAITING

Luke 12:11-12

Some say we live in an information age; skillful, accurate communication is essential—at work, in interpersonal relationships, even at play. Knowing what to say and how to say it is important for all of us.

For people of faith, though, finding the right words has always been a struggle. How can we, the finite, speak of the infinite?

Jesus reassured his disciples that if we abide in the Holy Spirit, somehow we will find the faith-full words. And doesn't *abide* mean to wait—as we ponder, puzzle, and brush up on our language skills?

We might express it this way:

> It was thus when immigrants came over
> And waited
> Without language
> As they embarked on new
> And uncertain land;
> All they knew for so long
> Was a room for waiting.

Living Word, may acts of faith follow stumbling words when all else fails. Amen.

Hymns: "O God, Our Help in Ages Past"
"Lord of All Hopefulness"

JUST THE ASHES?

1 Corinthians 11:23-26

When one of my colleagues in chaplaincy was observing Ash Wednesday with the imposition of ashes in the hospital chapel, he was confronted with an unusual request. A hospital employee approached the Communion rail, but did not kneel. As the chaplain came closer, expecting her to kneel, she gave no indication that she was going to do so.

She looked him directly in the eye and said, "Just the ashes. I'm in a hurry."

Our whole life is movement toward death. The ashes of our failures, sins, and dashed hopes indelibly mark us as mortal. So when the moment to reflect on our human condition is offered, we should pause long enough to appreciate the single death toward which we move—the death of Christ, which made possible the Death of all deaths.

Come, Lord Jesus!

Lord, when we move too quickly past your signs of grace, put up a roadblock at the next intersection of our lives. Amen.

Hymns: "O Jesus, I Have Promised"
　　　　"Come, Thou Fount of Every Blessing"

KNOWLEDGE OR FACT?

Luke 10:25-37

Alec J. Langford tells of giving a Bible quiz to boys in a reform school, and then later repeating the quiz with the young people at his own church. To his surprise, he found that the youth at his church, who had never been in court, never faced life away from families who loved them, and who had attended church and Sunday school from a young age, knew little more about the Bible than the boys in the state reform institution!

What conclusions can we draw from this story? Simply this: Possession of facts, even facts about the Bible, does not guarantee that a person will live up to the precepts presented there.

Two people recited the Twenty-third Psalm. Although both knew the words, it was obvious that only the second moved the people listening. When the pastor was asked the reason, he replied, "The first person knew the psalm, the second knew the Shepherd."

Remember the story of the rich young ruler. He had kept all the laws from his youth, but still something was lacking. Until we know the Shepherd, facts will not help us grow in grace, find peace, or know the joy of living for others and for God.

O gentle Shepherd, thank you for coming to live among us, to show us the way. We appreciate the facts of the Bible more because you have shown us how to use those facts to live our daily lives more fully. Amen.

Hymns: "Savior, Like a Shepherd Lead Us"
      "Seek Ye First the Kingdom of God"

JESUS LOVES ME

Ephesians 6:10-24

Look through a hymnal one day and take note of the many hymns about Jesus' love for us. For many of us, our faith statement can be summed up in those simple words we learned so long ago, "Jesus loves me! This I know, for the Bible tells me so."

As followers of the risen Lord, however, we cannot stop there. We have to ask, as in the hymn "We Are Climbing Jacob's Ladder," "Do you love my Jesus?" and, "If you love him, why not serve him?" for to love Jesus is to take up the cross and follow him. The sign of Christian greatness is how much one is willing to befriend those in need of a friend.

Jesus told us clearly the meaning of true friendship when he said:

Come, you that are blessed by my Father, inherit the kingdom prepared for you from the foundation of the world; for I was hungry and you gave me food, I was thirsty and you gave me something to drink, I was a stranger and you welcomed me, I was naked and you gave me clothing, I was sick and you took care of me, I was in prison and you visited me. (Matthew 25:34b-36)

Yes, Jesus does love me—just as he loved those that the world found so unlovely, the leper, the outcast, the weak, the poor. For us to show our love for Jesus, we must love our neighbor, whether in the town where we live or halfway around the world.

Great God, we praise you for the gift of your Son, Jesus. Be with us as we go through our days and help us always to be mindful of those who need a friend. Amen.

Hymns: "What a Friend We Have in Jesus"
        "Jesus, the Very Thought of Thee"

GOD SO LOVED THE WORLD

John 3

If you were asked to summarize the gospel in one verse, which would you offer? The verse most of us think of immediately is the one that Martin Luther called "the little gospel."

For God so loved the world that he gave his only Son, so that everyone who believes in him may not perish but may have eternal life. (John 3:16)

Here we see the essential statement of our faith: God loves this foolish, blundering, wayward, sin-sick world. God did not create the world and then leave the world to run by itself. No indeed, the Son of God left his heavenly home, came to dwell on earth, and is still today involved in the world's affairs.

God's love for this blundering world is beyond our understanding or human conception of what love means and is. The prophet Isaiah expressed it for us:

> *For my thoughts are not your*
> *thoughts,*
> *nor are your ways my ways,*
> *says the LORD.*

> *For as the heavens are higher*
> *than the earth,*
> *so are my ways higher than*
> *your ways*
> *and my thoughts than your thoughts. (Isaiah 55:8-9)*

By human standards, the gospel and this love of God are incredible upon the face of it.

How does God prove this love? God holds back nothing and could do no more than this. His was the supreme sacrifice—his Son. God could not let us go; so God's only Son came to earth, lived with us, and died for us. Now we know God's love, and in its power we are made whole.

O God, help us to live within the power of your great love, so that we might be made whole. Amen.

Hymns: "He Touched Me"
       "Stand By Me"

THE BUSY BEE

Galatians 6:1-10

A red clover blossom contains less than one-eighth of a grain of sugar. Yet seven thousand of these grains are required to make a pound of honey. A bee, therefore, must visit 56,000 clover heads to get enough sugar for a pound of honey. But there are about sixty flower tubes to each clover head. Thus the bee performs that operation 3,360,000 times to get enough sweetness for a single pound!

The truth is that most things worth doing take a lot of determination and plain persistence. Said Rousseau: "My manuscripts, blotted, scratched, interlined, and scarcely legible, attest the trouble they cost me." Said Montesquieu upon completing *The Spirit of Laws,* a work that influenced the framing of the United States Constitution: "You will read this treatise in a few hours, yet the labor expended on it has whitened my hair."

It is a principle that holds whatever our goal. Getting an education, for instance. Or having a really successful career. Or developing a strong personality. Or building a Christian character and home. These things don't come overnight. They come about only after countless minutes and hours and years of effort. A good name or a solid reputation grows slowly with the patient, daily blending of the right ingredients. These include such simple things as honesty, truthfulness, faith, and purity. If we are as wise as the bee, we will "not be weary in well doing" (Galatians 6:9 KJV). Great objectives require great perseverance.

In times of discouragement, O Lord, keep us from quitting our posts of duty and service. Amen.

Hymns: "Leaning on the Everlasting Arms"
   "Holy God, We Praise Thy Name"

CIVIC-MINDED

Psalm 15:1-5

Given the day of the week, the year, the season, the community, the right time and the right place, the highest honor bestowed upon anyone is to be called "a good citizen." To be a hero ranks a bit higher, but opportunities to be a real hero in our particular era and culture are severely limited. We are a generation struggling not to be cynical, skeptical, suspicious. It's a wonder that we still hope for a "good citizen," but we do, and still our prayers are answered.

This psalm says it all. Here is a description of that man or woman, girl or boy, whom we are looking for and always have need of in troubled times. Here is "Mr. Smith Goes to Washington" in your own backyard. We wish. We hope. We pray—for a citizen of integrity, truth; no slander, no evil to a neighbor, loyal to friends.

Read through the lens of Christian faith, we see the results of a forgiven life, a saved life, an abundant life. God knows that we *can't* do it in our natural uncivic-minded state. And God knows that doing all these things toward a good citizen "badge" will not make us right before God. The saved Christian knows it's a standard not likely to be maintained consistently. But, with the gospel, it is not unimaginable!

Lord of all, help us to be good citizens, for following your Word and your ways will lead to the paths of honor. Amen.

Hymns: "Lord, I Want to Be a Christian"
       "Lift High the Cross"

ATTENTION

Proverbs 1:24, 25

Attention, shoppers." Those two words, bursting through the piped-in music in a department store, are guaranteed to get your attention. You might be comparing prices on cans of green beans, completely focused on your household budget, but hear those two words, "Attention, shoppers," and a bargain, a sale, a reduced price, is all it takes to demolish a well-thought-out shopping list!

It is amazing how we hear what we want to hear! Even in a world of constant messages—buy this, see me, go there, do this, be that—we choose from hundreds of possibilities each week. But how often do we pay attention to the word of wisdom? How often do we hear a message that speaks to growing as a person, to feeding your soul with heavenly, good, eternal water?

Proverbs says, "No one paid attention." Read on and you will find the consequences of ignoring wisdom! It is enough to send you back to list-making before you go shopping!

Eternal Wisdom, open my eyes and ears to your Word, while I tune out the many words of my many worlds. Amen.

Hymns: "Open My Eyes"
　　　　"Take Time to Be Holy"

THE COLLECTOR

Joshua 24:14-25

Some of us are like the man who found a dollar lying on the ground. From then on he kept looking for things. He always kept his eyes on the road when he walked. At the end of forty years, he had picked up 34,947 buttons, 54,712 pins, 11 pennies, a bent back, and a bad disposition! At the same time, he had lost the glory of the sun, the smiles of friends, the beauties of nature, and the chance to serve others.

It seems that most of us keep looking for something for nothing. It gets to be a mania. But the world is not made that way. The greatest treasures of happiness and well-being come to those who work the hardest, give the most, and serve the best. This is a law of life and of God. If we decide to collect pins, we may get a few free baubles, but we are likely to lose our souls.

The choice is ours, in spite of what anyone says. We are free to decide whether we will pick up pins or follow the stars. As a rule, when we look for something for nothing, we get nothing. When we give more than we need to, we usually get more than we need. This is God's way for us.

Thank God we are free to choose, even though sometimes we choose poorly. It is up to us. We live in a world of bewildering choices. God pity us if we decide to collect buttons instead of blessings!

When we choose, dear Lord, may our choices be in keeping with thy will for us. Amen.

Hymns: "Freely, Freely"
       "O How I Love Jesus"

THE TWO SAPPHIRES

Psalm 119:65-72

A contestant on a TV program was asked to choose between two star sapphires. One was a natural stone, worth $5,000. The other was created in a lab and was worth $500. She was to keep the one she chose, and unfortunately, she chose the imitation.

That is the way with many of us. There are so many things that look good to us. The cheap stuff is made to look like the real thing. Sometimes it takes an expert to tell the difference. And we often get taken because we don't have a basis to judge. We are easy marks for phony goods made to resemble the actual article.

It is that way also in trying to decide about people and ideas and values by which to live. So often the shoddy is dressed up and polished to look nice. We need some help to enable us to distinguish the good from the bad. The moral laws of God and the teachings of Jesus are tested and trustworthy guides to help us make a "right judgment in all things." The prayer of the psalmist might well be ours: "Teach me good judgment." If we seek such help honestly, and are willing to use it, we will find that it never fails. If our intent is good we rarely are let down.

Of course, life always involves risks of one kind or another. Some choices are not clear-cut, but we reduce the danger of guesswork as we rely on divine values.

Guide our minds and hearts, O God, so that we may separate the good from the bad, the real from the false. In Christ's name. Amen.

Hymns: "He Is Lord"
       "I Know Whom I Have Believed"

DON'T BUMP YOUR HEAD!

Matthew 7:13-20

One of the highways entering Chicago goes under a railroad bridge. The overpass carries the warning, "Clearance 11 feet, 11 inches." A closer look reveals that there had been a sign that read "Clearance 12 feet." The edge of the concrete is chipped away where trucks with higher loads had tried to get through. The new sign is an admission of a fact of life. One inch can make a big difference.

There is a parable here for the business of living. Too many of us like to think we can defy the plain laws of the universe and of the human race and get away with it. It is well and good to think tall and plan big, to try to carry as heavy a load as possible. Unfortunately, we often overdo it. We are not superhuman. We can't make the world over to suit our plans. We can't take things into our own hands and not expect to get our heads bumped.

As children of God we must accept God's laws and the world as it is. A feeling of self-superiority can get us into trouble. The way is narrow that leads to life. It also is likely to have a low ceiling. Most of us need to learn the humility of the bowed head, but there are few who do so.

Dear Lord, give us the wisdom from above to know what we should do and the willingness to be content to do it. In Jesus' name. Amen.

Hymns: "Thy Word Is a Lamp"
       "My Faith Looks Up to Thee"

WINDY CORNERS

Psalm 100

There is a formation known as Angel Rock on the eastern slope of the San Jacinto mountain range in California. Viewed from the plain below, these stones take the form of a great angel above the city of Palm Springs. Someone has pointed out that Angel Rock can best be seen from a point on Highway 99 known as Windy Corners. It is here that galelike winds often whip from the ocean through the narrow pass. Yet from that very point, Angel Rock may best be seen.

Life is like that. Most of us are no strangers to Windy Corners. Yet when the winds blow the hardest, we can look up and get our clearest view of the overarching providence of God. It is strange but true that sometimes it takes suffering to make us aware at last of the presence and love of God. In a time of crisis or trouble we may be the most sure that God is always standing by, just as he was standing by when Jesus died on the cross.

When our minds fail to understand, when our strength gives out, when our hearts are crushed and broken, the infinite love of God is ready to reach out and gather us in. Why turn away from God at our time of most need? With God at our side, we have no need to fear Windy Corners.

O God, Healer of the bruised and the broken, in our worst possible circumstances remind us that you are near. Amen.

Hymns: "Lord of the Dance"
        "Beneath the Cross of Jesus"

ON GOING TO THE PEN

Luke 13:1-5

In the early days of the Christian church the admission of wrong-doing as a start toward doing better was stressed a great deal. The person who wanted to make amends for sins often was given something to do as a penance. For instance, that person might be required to spend forty hours in prayer or to fast three days in absolute silence. It was hard for people to do these things in their normal surroundings, so many churches set aside a room for the use of penitents. It was natural to call this a penitentiary. After many centuries, this term came to describe a place to put lawbreakers.

In these modern days it might be well to revive this earlier meaning of penitentiary. If we did, our prisons might not be so crowded. Most of our sins are not due to sickness or to bad environments. We sin because our hearts are greedy, lustful, envious, and hateful. We sin because we think we are wiser than God. We think God's moral laws somehow don't apply to us.

In spite of our excuses, however, we still need to repent of our sins and claim the cleansing power of God in the gospel of Christ. This is the way to life and freedom. It would do all of us good to spend some time in the "pen."

Everlasting God, we humbly seek your divine forgiveness for our sins of the spirit that shut us away from you. By your mercy, make us clean, whole, and happy again. Amen.

Hymns: "Rock of Ages, Cleft for Me"
　　　 "Because He Lives"

THE CHRONOMETER

John 14:1-14

The use of longitude is a necessary aid to navigation. The secret of longitude lies in an accurate clock called a chronometer. Early navigators did not have such a clock, and countless lives and many valuable ship cargoes were lost as a result of inaccurate steering. In the early eighteenth century, the British Parliament offered an award of twenty thousand pounds (about $32,000 in today's money) to anyone who discovered a device that would enable a ship's longitude to be found. Hundreds tried and failed.

Clockmaker John Harrison began working on the problem when he was twenty-one and finished at the age of sixty-six. At long last sailors could find their location anywhere in the world. With a dependable standard they were freed from the terror of the unknown.

As we make our journeys through unknown years, we too need a dependable guide, a chronometer to give location and direction. We find it in Jesus Christ. Without him many lives are lost and much talent wasted. In him we find our perfect chronometer to give us our bearings and show us the way.

In Jesus we find that the center of the universe is not nothingness or abstract ideas or matter or force. It is rather a loving God who finds us wherever we are and directs us home. "I am the way." We are never lost on the open seas of philosophy, materialism, science. Jesus is a dependable guide for all voyagers. Jesus frees us from fear of the unknown.

Almighty God, direct our decisions so that we may always choose the right way. Save us from easy compromises and keep us on the upward path. Amen.

Hymns: "Victory in Jesus"
        "Blessed Assurance"

WE ARE NOT ALONE

Ephesians 2:11-22

"Our Father . . . "

The first word of the Lord's Prayer assures us that when we approach God we are never alone. The first word also warns us that we cannot approach God except as we are related to the family of God. Jesus teaches us to pray not "My Father" but "*Our* Father." We pray as members of a fellowship that shares the love of God with one another. We pray not as isolated individuals but as members of a new community in which the loneliness of the self-serving ego has been transcended.

After a class of six-year-old children had visited the worship service of their church, they were asked, "What did you like most about being in church?" Quickly one of the little girls replied, "The Lord's Prayer!" When asked "Why?" she hugged herself and replied, "Because it felt so good to hear us all say it together." She had begun to experience what it means to say, "Our Father."

Whether in the midst of a large congregation or alone in our room, we pray surrounded by those with whom we share the love of God, surrounded as well by those who suffer and die in war or famine, those humiliated by prejudice or crippled by poverty, ignorance, or illness.

Help us break through the walls of our isolation, to gather us together and teach us to say, "Our Father." Amen.

Hymns: "Sing Praise to God Who Reigns Above"
"Guide Me, O Thou Great Jehovah"

DESIRED JOY

John 6:27-35

Ihad prepared to "speak a piece" as a first grader in the Sunday-school Christmas program. The subject was "Presents." As I stepped forward to rehearse, my teacher handed me a small gift-wrapped package. Thinking that it was for me, I thanked her profusely. How deflated I felt when she informed me that it was just an empty box, a prop for my presentation.

How many times we experience the same letdown after getting something we wanted and thought we really needed. "The Joy of Our Desiring," in the words of the familiar hymn, is not to be realized by the acquisition of most of the things for which we labor so hard. A better car, a better position, a bigger house—after the initial thrill—are like gift-wrapped empty boxes. They are not able to satisfy our desires. Jesus warns us not to labor for food that perishes but for the food that endures.

This food is the daily bread for which we pray. Jesus is that bread. Jesus is our joy. "I am," he said, "the bread of life." We should focus our desires not on beautifully wrapped packages, empty inside, but on the gift of life, as plain and as nourishing as an unwrapped chunk of bread.

We desire so many things, O Lord of Life, yet when we find them, we are unsatisfied and desire more. Lead us to the feast you have prepared. Feed us till we want no more. Amen.

Hymns: "Christ, from Whom All Blessings Flow"
        "Bread of the World"

TRUE FORGIVENESS

Matthew 6:9-15

Many years ago a world-famous engineer, Peer Holm, who had known wealth and fame, fell into poverty and was forced to return with his wife and small daughter to the village where he was born.

His neighbor, an old man, had a fierce dog. Peer knew that the dog was dangerous, but the old man refused to listen to his pleas to keep the dog locked up. One day Peer returned home and, to his horror, found the dog attacking his little girl. He tore the dog away, but not in time to save his daughter's life.

The village turned against the old man. His dog was shot. When the time for sowing came, no one would sell him seed. But Peer could not sleep at night. So early one morning he rose, took the last half-bushel of his barley, climbed the fence to his neighbor's field, and sowed the seed. When the time came for the first shoots to appear, others learned of Peer's act of forgiveness. While part of his fields lay bare, his neighbor's field was green.

We have that capacity for forgiveness when we realize that, while deserving the harshest judgment for our faithlessness, we have been given instead the generous sign of God's forgiving love. Knowing that we are forgiven, we can forgive.

O God, never let us forget your great love for us. May our love for you be revealed by our loving forgiveness of others. Amen.

Hymns: "Jesus, the Very Thought of Thee"
       "Love Divine, All Loves Excelling"

SCRIBES, PHARISEES, AND US

Matthew 5:17-48

Jesus knew that the scribes and Pharisees were righteous people. He knew that by every human standard they were also excellent people—serious-minded, public-spirited, highly moral and ethical in their dealings, careful and punctual in their religious observances. They were people we would be honored to have in our homes, yet Jesus often rebuked them. Why?

These righteous ones, the guardians of religion and morality, were strong in their own strength. They sought to earn their salvation. They did not come to God as sinners asking forgiveness as a gift. Strong in themselves, they could not love God or the sinners around them because they did not know the meaning of divine forgiveness. Their religion was correct, moral, law-abiding. It was also without spontaneity—anxious, dull, humorless, and narrow. Too often this religion was a series of *don'ts*, an adherence to the letter of the law, to the neglect of the life-giving Spirit. It was a religion that repelled sinners.

And we? How easy it is to condemn the scribes and Pharisees! But let us ask ourselves if our righteousness turns away any desperate, bitter person seeking a new start. Do our morality and goodness repel? Let us repent of our repelling goodness and accept God's forgiveness and goodness.

May your love, O Lord, always be found in our hearts. Amen.

Hymns: "When I Survey the Wondrous Cross"
"Come, Christians, Join to Sing"

JESUS' STRANGE COMPANY

Matthew 9

Jesus was known by the company he kept—all who needed him: the despised tax collectors, down-and-outers, the mentally deranged, women who needed to recover their lost womanhood, rulers of the people, paralytics, children. He sought the company of some odd characters.

Aren't we glad for that fact? We who have been taught to watch the company we keep? We are often reminded to shun the appearance of evil. Jesus asks us to be far more concerned with real evil than with the appearance of it. We fear for our reputations, should we be caught associating with "those people." Is our religion so shallow and timid that we view such associations as a threat?

Our attitudes may repel the very persons we are trying to reach for Christ—the very persons who need to experience the love of Christ. It is easy for us to lift our hands in horror, as the religious leaders of Jesus' day did when they saw him enjoying himself at a banquet in the company of sinners who had been ostracized. What a scandal! To add insult to injury, he told the righteous critics that tax collectors and harlots would enter the kingdom of God before these critics. Why? The critics were loveless.

O great Teacher, your kingdom is built on infinite love. Heal us and instruct us until we see your image in all people—for you died for all. Amen.

Hymns: "Holy God, We Praise Thy Name"
       "This Is My Father's World"

SIGNS OF THE COVENANT

Genesis 9:8-17

Someone once asked William Blake what he saw when the sun rose. The poet replied, "I see an immeasurable company of the heavenly host crying, 'Holy, Holy, Holy is the Lord God almighty.'"

What do you see when a rainbow appears in the sky—a gorgeous arc in the clouds or a sign of God's covenant with us?

After suffering the terrors of the Flood, Noah had wondered whether life would endure. He questioned the dependability of nature and God. Then in the heavens a rainbow appeared. As a warrior lays aside his weapon in token that warfare has ceased, so God had hung the rainbow in the clouds. The lightning had stopped, and there in the sky was the reminder of God's faithfulness, God's enduring covenant.

As in Noah's day, so now God puts signs around us. Springtime comes, seedtime, and harvest. The rainbow is the sign, one among thousands in nature alone, that God is faithful.

We need these signs today. We need to hope. In hope, God continually discloses himself to us.

Eternal Spirit, we praise you for the hope that does not disappoint us; we see the signs of it daily. Amen.

Hymns: "Holy, Holy, Holy"
       "How Great Thou Art"

GOD'S SURENESS

Mark 4:21-29

Y ou plant corn in your garden, turn your back on it for a few days, and you find blades breaking through the ground. If you look at the corn every day, the growth from day to day may seem slow. A few days away from the garden will reveal astounding growth. The whole order of nature is working to produce the full grain, and because the earth works as it does, growth and harvest are sure.

So it is with the kingdom of God, said Jesus. Just as we watch the earth produce its grain, so we watch the Kingdom. We work with God, but the basic growth process and the outcome are not in our control. Because God works as God does, growth is certain. God's kingdom is near us, around us, within us, and above us—all this we may know, just as surely as we know the garden's growth in spring and summer.

Jesus' parable speaks especially to parents and teachers. Who has not known the experience of investing time in a young person, cooperating with God, and then after a time seeing the astonishing results? Every school commencement dramatizes the truth of Jesus' words. God works unceasingly in the lives of us all.

Because your love is everlasting and has been evidenced in us over the changing years, we turn in confidence to you, O Lord. Amen.

Hymns: "A Mighty Fortress Is Our God"
         "He Is Lord"

WATCH!

Matthew 24

It is possible to be so preoccupied with speculations concerning the Second Coming that we may miss Christ's presence here and now. Perhaps that is why some of us become impatient with people who comb the New Testament for verses that seem to predict the timing of the Second Coming.

Our reading for today encourages no idle speculation. Jesus counsels an attitude of watchfulness—an attitude that must characterize our lives daily. His words are not designed for some vague time in the future. Their emphasis is NOW.

Watch! Be ready. Don't miss God.

A couple were discussing a trip to the American West. The husband described a breathtaking view of a canyon. His wife said to him, "I never saw that." He replied, "Of course, you didn't—you were looking from the wrong side of the train!"

Jesus teaches us that our God is the God of surprises. God may come like a thief in the night. We must keep our eyes open, be characterized by a careful attention so that we may not miss the manifestations of God in our lives and in the lives of those around us.

O Lord, touch our eyes so that we see you in our daily lives, and having seen you, turn to serving you. Amen.

Hymns: "Jesu, Jesu"
      "The Voice of God Is Calling"

GIFTS TO BE USED

Matthew 25:1-30

*N*othing ventured, nothing gained. That is a maxim we often hear. Our reading for today might be translated a little differently: *Nothing ventured, everything lost.*

Jesus is reminding us that our talents are God's gifts to be used. If you have five talents and you make use of them, you may find yourself with ten talents. If I have one talent and I bury it, even that talent will be lost.

Jesus asks us to venture, to take the risk of committing our talents to him. That is the only kind of life that makes sense—and brings joy.

We see how this works daily. Muscles unused become flabby and fail. A person learns a language, ceases to use it, and the language is no longer a living part of him. An individual opens her life to a friendship but retreats in distrust and fear, and the friendship dissipates in indifference or hostility. In each case, the original gift is lost.

Jesus reminds us to use the talents we have, to live in faith, to venture with courage. Then he assures us that ultimately, we cannot fail.

Gracious God, we ask your forgiveness for the many times we have hidden our talents away. Help us each day to use our gifts in your service. Amen.

Hymns: "Something Beautiful"
       "El Shaddai"

A BETTER LANGUAGE

Matthew 20:1-16

There must have been a lot of chatter around the table in the house of Simon, and perhaps not much was really being said. Jesus was facing death, and he had not been able to communicate fully with his disciples because they would not hear him. Then a woman appeared. Utter silence fell over the room. In silence she poured ointment on Jesus' head. She was anointing his body for burial.

She spoke more eloquently in this act than could a thousand sermons. Her actions bore a personal meaning for those present—she said to all, "Let us respond to the infinite love of God extended to us in this lowly man, our Savior. Let us give because grace to us has been given."

And Jesus responded. This act was a thing of beauty. From the abundance of her heart the woman's hands spoke. Hers was a sacramental touch that consecrates a body soon to be broken.

Her act echoes down through the centuries. In it nothing was wasted. By it the hungry and poor are fed. Through this act, Jesus speaks again to us of the Father's eternal love.

> Bread of the world in mercy broken,
> Wine of the soul in mercy shed,
> By whom the words of life were spoken,
> And in whose death our sins are dead.
>
> *Reginald Heber, 1827*

Hymns: "Become to Us the Living Bread"
"Here, O My Lord, I See Thee"

OLD TESTAMENT RELIGION

Jeremiah 31:1-6

We hear people speak of the religion of the Old Testament being a religion of laws and the religion of the New Testament being a religion of love. But the religion of the Old Testament is also a religion of love—steadfast, eternal love, love that is particular and focused.

We survey best the mountain range when we stand at the pinnacle. This applies in all endeavors, not just in mountain climbing. For Christians, the summit of Old Testament religion is contained in the majestic passages of Jeremiah, Isaiah, Hosea, the Psalms, and others that tell us of the steadfast love of God that endures forever.

From its beginnings as a nation, Israel knew the presence of God in every event of its history, knew *grace in the wilderness* after surviving the sword of Pharaoh. *From afar* the Lord appeared to his people—high and lifted up, as from Mt. Sinai, he bridged the gap between eternal love and human sin and need.

"Jeremiahs" they are called when we want to describe gloomy, fainthearted, and frightened leaders today. But we repeat a stereotype. We miss the incomparable courage, joy, and optimism of the magnificent prophet who, in the darkest time, bought some land and called the young to take timbrels and dance.

I have loved you with an everlasting love. . . . For God so loved the world . . . therefore, O Lord, in the old and new covenants, you have said everything to us. Grant us to live on that. Amen.

Hymns: "More Love to Thee, O Christ"
"Be Thou My Vision"

DISASTER, YET . . .

Habakkuk

Pack up your troubles . . . and smile, smile, smile." "Smile and the world smiles with you." Amusing counsel, and perhaps superficially helpful, but these old sayings do not offer much solid help when we confront the enormous power of evil. Habakkuk gives more timely help.

God rules the world, yet God allows violence, injustice, and oppression to overwhelm the righteous. Why? Habakkuk answers our question: You shall live by being faithful. Keep your head. Do right, whatever comes; and trust that God will bring about the best result in good time. Look for God's revelation amid your woes, and be assured that evil will not have the last word. Live by daring trust and commitment to God, who does not fail.

The prophet cites some frightful worries that plague the just. These, he says, bear the fruit of their own destruction. Yet, he will rejoice in God, who saves him now.

Faith, then, does not pack up our troubles and bid us smile. It drives us into them with courage and leads us to rejoice, because the right has triumphed in us and allied us with the power that ultimately will win over all evil.

Help us, O Lord, to live by faith—in daily thanksgiving, in daily trust, and in the abiding joy that confidence in you always brings. Amen.

Hymns: "O for a Thousand Tongues to Sing"
"I'll Praise My Maker While I've Breath"

ARE YOU THERE?

Deuteronomy 30:11-20

A re you there? Sometimes when the conversation falls dead on the phone, we ask this. Or one person may say it to break another's absorption in the newspaper. It really says: I am present to you, but are you present to me?

Moses discussed this question on a larger scale when he spoke to the Israelites. The people, he said, must live in covenant with the God who is present. To communicate with God, they do not need to understand the vast mysteries of life. God is with them as a personal presence. God's Word is in their hearts.

Religious revelation, therefore, is not a striving for the impossible. It comes as we respond to God, who extends love and who is there. Science helps us discover new truths about our physical world. But the most simple person can experience the revelation of God by being present—being open and receptive to God's love.

Though none of us can comprehend the mystery of God's being, any of us can experience God revealed through love. God's revelation is at hand—in God's love, correction, and care expressed to us through the creation; through our history; and through the One who lived among us, died, and rose again. In these communications, God summons us to attention. Are we there?

Dear God, help us to be more aware of your presence within us, around us, and beyond us. Help us to be present to you and to others. Amen.

Hymns: "O Worship the King"
       "All People That on Earth Do Dwell"

"WHERE IS THE GOD OF JUSTICE?"

Malachi 2:17—3:12

Wars. Worldwide hunger. Slums. Oppression of the poor, of racial and religious minorities. Organized cheating and robbing of the public. Where in all this is the God of justice? Can we escape this question as we read our daily newspaper or watch TV?

Malachi, messenger of God's justice and reform, deals with this question. People have complained to him about God's injustice. He replies that God will come to right the wrongs they complain about. Meanwhile, let the people be about the business of correcting the evils for which they are responsible. God is offended by the spiritual corruption evidenced in the violations of the temple, but God is most deeply insulted by the sins against the children of God—the hired worker, the widow and orphan, the sojourner. God's judgment will fall upon those who oppress the weak. God is neither indifferent nor powerless to right human wrongs.

Like all Old Testament prophets, Malachi looks forward. He presents the idea of a forerunner who will right injustices in preparation for God's appearing. The church has seen John the Baptist as this forerunner of the ministry of the Messiah.

Where is the God of justice? Acting daily in history, as Malachi reported. We may be blind to this action or not. God came to us decisively in Jesus Christ, who identifies himself with the poor, the humiliated, and the oppressed, and who calls us to right the wrongs around us.

Grant us, O God, your grace. Help us to be about the business of correcting the evils for which we are responsible. Amen.

Hymns: "Amazing Grace"
"Grace Greater Than Our Sin"

A QUOTE TO REMEMBER

Acts 20:17-38

It is more blessed to give than to receive.—Acts 20:35b

Paul is speaking his last words to the church leaders at Ephesus. United to them by deep personal bonds of affection, he has lived, worked, and suffered with them to spread the good news. Now, in a decision that reminds us of Jesus' resolve to go up to Jerusalem, Paul is ready to break with the life here with his friends. He too will go to Jerusalem, where his future will be decided.

Paul reminds the leaders of the life they have had together and how he has always been honest with them in facing common problems. He anticipates trouble in the future. He knows he will not see these friends again. What does he say? He tells them to guard the truth of the good news, and he leaves them with a quote, a special word for a special occasion: It is more blessed to give than to receive.

These are the words of Jesus, words that do not appear in the Gospels but words that reveal the heart of the good news. Jesus' whole life confirms the words. Paul, whose one purpose is to follow in the steps of Jesus, goes up to Jerusalem and leaves the church at Ephesus with this legacy: Give—yourself, your talents, your material means, because God in Christ has given everything to you.

O Lord, because we have first received, we ask you for grace to build our lives upon a commitment to give. Amen.

Hymns: "Hope of the World"
      "Stand Up, Stand Up for Jesus"

JESUS REMEDIES OUR BUSYNESS

Luke 18:15-17

When the disciples began to seem 'busy,'" wrote Kierkegaard, "Christ set a child in their midst."

We do not know what the disciples were doing when this happened. Perhaps they were restructuring their committees, setting up new task forces, or studying their public relations image. Whatever they were doing, Jesus said to them by his action that they should make room for the revelation of God in their midst. God's kingdom was not to be found in the overly busy activities of the disciples. Nowhere did Jesus say that blessed are the work-obsessed, the corporate martyrs whose hours are overlong and tedious because their gospel is work.

While Jesus is dealing with conditions for entering the kingdom of heaven, some mothers bring children to him for his blessing. In their pride and impatience, the disciples rebuke the children, but Jesus tells the disciples they must become as little children or they will miss the kingdom of God altogether. And what are little children noted for? They are imaginative, sensitive to what is going on about them, frank, humble. They live in an atmosphere of trust, wonder, enchantment, openness, adventure. In such an environment, God's kingdom comes.

O God, who came to us as child and teacher—our example and Savior—help us to become as little children, that we may not miss your kingdom. Amen.

Hymns: "Jesus Loves Me"
       "Tell Me the Stories of Jesus"

HANDS

Psalm 24:1-6

There are several things we can do with our hands. We can wring them in despair and bitterness. Handwringers think the world is against them. They are sure everything is all wrong. They are afraid and unhappy. Then, too, we can clench our hands. We can double up our fists in hate. We can always be suspicious and spiteful and fussy. We can be greedy and selfish, interested only in grabbing things for ourselves.

On the other hand, we can open our hands in friendship, love, and service. We can give a helping hand to someone in need. We can set our open hands to useful work to help make a better world. Best of all, we can clasp our hands in prayer. When we turn to God in sincerity and honesty, God never turns away. Praying hands mean clean hands and a pure heart. Prayer brings us forgiveness, peace, and power for the living of our days.

We would be happier, and, yes, better Christians if we quit wringing and clenching our hands and tried opening them in service and clasping them in prayer.

Cleanse our hearts, O God, that we may honor you with the work of our hands. Amen.

Hymns: "Every Time I Feel the Spirit"
   "Where He Leads Me"